MW01241340

///// thanks /////

Chris Bick / Melissa Bierstock / Kate Bingaman–Burt / Anne Brandt / Jill Bressler / Jacinta Bunnell / Brenna Chase / Hayley Downs / K Greene / Natalie Holland / Jamie Kennard/ Marci Kiehl / Sean Miller / Diana Mosbacher / Annie Poon / Brian Ricci / Véronique Schwob / Jenne Skye / Juliet Towne / Olivia Venier / Lonna Whiting / Carmen Willenbring

for
You_

About
this
book
series_

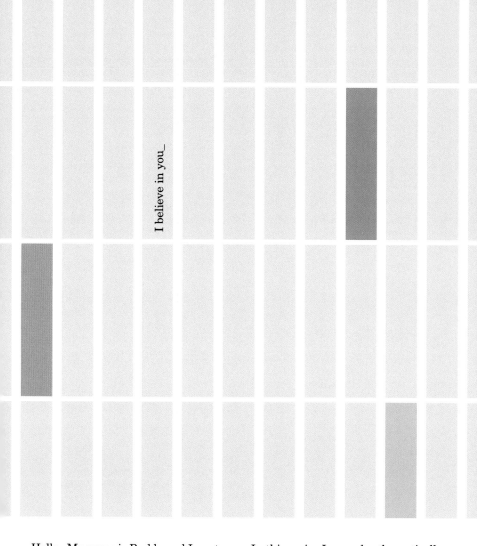

I believe in you_

Hello_ My name is Buddy and I wrote this book! On every page/ every word/ I thought about you_ I hope you/re well_ If by chance you/re not feeling so great/ though/ I hope I can help_ This is my goal in life_

Rainbows is about improving your mood/ full of suggestions large and small – and I promise many ideas will take less than five minutes – to help you better enjoy today_ I won/t recommend anything that I haven/t tried myself and also I/ll snazz this up with personal stories/ rad art and graphics/ playlists and more_

In this series I use color thematically to organize mood turnaround tips in small doses_ There are ten chapters/ ten colors > black / blue / pink / yellow / green / purple / brown / orange / red / white_ Start wherever you like_

Note that silver is not on the list_ I love that color!! but want to mention that nothing in these books is a silver bullet_ Instead/ it/s the combination of small efforts and your willingness to keep trying that that will take you anywhere you dream_

I love you/

Buddy

5

It/s not easy bein/ green_

At the beginning of this year I had a relapse of depression/ the worst I/d had in 30 years_ It was awful_ I was in hell_Looking in the mirror I didn/t recognize myself_ Listening to music hurt_ Seeing event flyers in shop windows hurt cuz people were doing things and going places and I was doing nothing and going nowhere_ I quit *Rainbows_*

I/m mentioning this because I don/t want you to give up_ I wanted to again and again/ for months/ but I just held on and eventually it did get better_ Omg it took forever but slowly I came back to myself_ I could see things again/ could work on the computer/ could write this book_ I never thought I could do it again but I did_ You can/ too_

When you are depressed/ people say it won/t last forever and I promise you it/s true_ I didn/t believe it but my good friend Annie kept reminding me_ She would call me every morning and take me out for a walk_ Most days that was the only thing that got me out of bed_ And I don/t think I would have made it through if it weren/t for Chris/ who let me stay with him when things got really bad_

What did I learn / re–learn from this experience? I learned how supportive my family and friends are_ You are not alone and you can/t do it alone_ You take that for granted sometimes_ I learned that forcing myself to do things/ even for only 5 minutes/ helps me feel better_ I rediscovered how cleaning my apartment improves my mood_

Many of these things we/ll explore in this chapter_ Some may resonate with you/ some may not_ However you/re feeling/ I encourage you to keep trying mood improvement activities that you haven/t tried before_ As the < heteronormative > saying goes/ one has to kiss a lot of frogs to find a handsome prince_

After months of hell/ I had one day where I enjoyed two good/ productive hours_ This gave me hope_ Perhaps I could do that again_ It/s taken time to build on it but I/m getting there_

The experience renewed my gratitude for simple things_ In Spring the flowers began to bloom and I felt grateful for that/ even though it still hurt a little bit_ I felt grateful for my small office where I write/ grateful for friends/ for dumb things like Diet Coke_ Most of all/ I feel grateful to be alive/ even though it hurts a lot_

Go for a walk_

Exercise is one of the most important things you can do to fight depression_ Walking – even small steps to the corner and back – absolutely counts_ A short walk can help just as much as a gym workout_ Why? Because walking is magic/ a simple way to get the body and mind moving_

Get outside and go for a walk_ Visit somewhere green and choose a path_ You are/ at this very moment/ on the right path_ Try to focus outward instead of inward_ Take in the trees/ the sun and shadow/ the sound of one foot in front of the other_

I have a game to distract myself from rehashing my problems > I actually narrate my experience/ like a tour guide_ I look at a flower_ In my mind I say/ There is a flower_ I look at a leaf/ then say/ There is a leaf_ I wander_ I observe_ I catalog_

I take deep inhale/exhales as the tour progresses/ almost as if I/m breathing in each detail_ The journey can be both comforting and eye–opening_ Somehow when I look/ really look/ or listen/ really listen/ I notice things I never have before_ < See the BLUE chapter/ pg_16 for more on this mindfulness technique_ >

It/s not a perfect system but at its best the running narration means less rumination_ I focus my senses on the present to let go of my worries about the future_

After all/ my mood won/t improve by worrying about it_ It/s the actions I take that will lead me towards recovery_ So I take a small step and then I take another_ I take a step after that and then a step after that_ That/s all you have to do_

Matt Green has walked every block of NYC_

interview >

Since 2011/ Matt Green has walked every street/ every block/ in every borough of NYC/ over 9000 miles_ His journey is the subject of the film *The World Before Your Feet_* Green/ who previously walked across the US from New York to Oregon/ has lots to say about the art of walking_

Describe a difficult time in your life and how walking helped you_
All through college and into my career as a civil engineer/ I had no idea what I wanted to do with my life_ That feeling of being lost and directionless while simultaneously moving along a career path that I didn/t want to be on was really painful/ because it felt like I was getting deeper and deeper into a life that I didn/t want_ The further along I went/ the harder it became to imagine finding a way out of that life_ I always had different half–baked ideas about other careers I could have/ but it just seemed too difficult to do anything different/ and so I kept going back to work every day without ever changing anything_

In 2010 I finally broke out of my rut when I started thinking about the possibility of walking across America_ I gave myself a year to find a job that I liked/ and if I didn/t find one/ I would have to quit and walk across the country_ I started telling friends about my plan/ but I didn/t really think I would end up doing the walk_ A year felt like so much time/ and surely I could find a job I liked before the clock ran out_

But the months ticked by and/ of course/ I never got serious about finding another job_ I just kept going to work every day like I always had_ Before I knew it/ it had been a full year since I made the deal with myself_ Fortunately/ telling all my friends about the idea kept me honest_ It would have been a lot easier to go back on my word if I were the only one who knew about it_ And so I did quit my job and I did walk across America/ from Rockaway Beach/ New York to Rockaway Beach/ Oregon_

Sometimes people take big journeys like that in hopes of finding a miracle solution to their life/s problems_ Like you would just walk and walk and then some life-changing insight would fall from the heavens_ But that rarely happens/ and it didn/t happen with me_ What did happen/ however/ was the kind of slow–building change that/s almost too gradual to notice_ Every day I would get up/ pack my stuff into the cart < a reconfigured

jogging stroller > I was pushing/
walk a little bit farther west/ and
then start trying to figure out
where I would camp for the night/
which usually involved knocking
on strangers/ doors and asking if I
could sleep on their lawns_ Without
realizing what I was doing – I was
just trying to have an adventure – I
had entered a life that was much
simpler and more connected to
my needs as a human_ Traveling
on foot/ finding food and water/
looking for shelter – this was a life
with clear/ practical/ achievable
goals/ and a life that required
paying attention to the world/ to
my surroundings and my fellow
humans_

There weren/t a lot of material
comforts on my walk_ I spent most
nights in a tent/ ate what I could
afford from grocery stores and gas
stations < although the people
whose doors I knocked on looking
for places to stay provided me with
a surprising number of hot meals as
well > and basically wore the same
two sets of clothes over and over_
But I found myself so much happier
and more content than I had ever
been before_ Looking back on that
time now/ I think I was coming to a
new understanding of what being a
human is all about_

My walk reacquainted me with the
sense of humanity that we have
when we are children/ the idea
that life is about exploration and
learning/ about being connected to
the world and the untold beings that
we share it with_ It/s a beautiful
feeling to be out discovering things_

So after saying all that/ I also have
to say that I think I/m still just
as directionless as I was in my
engineering days_ It/s just that I
now understand there/s nothing
wrong with being directionless_
We/ve got enough directions in this
world as it is/ maybe we need more
people trying to exist where they

are instead of always trying to get
somewhere else_ And if that sounds
hypocritical coming from someone
who/s always out walking around/
cut me some slack/ I/m speaking
metaphorically!

In the film you express uncertainty
as to the point of your current
project of walking all of NYC and
that you are finding it out as you go_
What did you find out?
I still have no idea what the point
is_ Except that I think the point is
that it/s okay to not have a point_
It/s good to embrace pointlessness_
Not everything has to have some
clear goal_ Sometimes it/s good
to just do something you feel like
doing_ If you follow a goal that
means something to you/ your own
interest and curiosity can sustain
you and provide a sense of purpose/
and you/re not so dependent on the
approval of others to make you feel
worthwhile_

Why is walking important?
I/ve used this word a couple times
already/ but > Connection! We/re too
isolated_ We need more connection_
When you walk/ you/re present
in all the places you/re walking
through_ You/re not ensconced
inside a vehicle_ You/re immersed in
your surroundings_ You/re moving/
but you/re going slowly enough to
observe and to participate_ You see
the details/ you hear the sounds/
you feel the weather_ The world
becomes one continuous home/ not
just a set of discrete places that
you visit_ Plus it just feels good to
be outside moving around_ Maybe
that/s the real/ simple truth of it all_
Be outside_ Move around_

Annie Poon

12

Geocaching_

No one in the room had heard of geocaching at that time so I/ll describe/ just in case > Geocaching is a global treasure hunt with secret finds pretty much everywhere/ in places you/d never imagine_ You kinda have to try it to understand it so check out geocaching.com and download the app_ You/ll then use your phone/s navigation tools to find hidden caches large and small_ Their site beautifully explains/ There/s an adventure happening all the time/ all around you_

One evening a friend and I decided to try it_ We looked on the site to see if any caches might be nearby and discovered one on the map just down the street/ at the corner of Dusty Road and Nowhere_ We went immediately to try/ looking < not sure where to look > and inspecting < not sure what to expect > and combing the brush/ the dirt/ the rocks/ the shade to eventually discover a tiny container holding a scroll of paper wrapped round a paperclip/ a log of those who had found it before us_ No one had in five years_ But we did_

Definitely try this activity with a friend because it/s fun as a team_ And if you/re not up for beginning an adventure like this right now/ at the very least look at the site to preview what you can uncover near you one day_ I/m hoping seeing treasures marked on maps will change your perspective on things_ There are secrets all around_ Go find them!

What if I sent you a secret message in this book? What if every green letter on this page created a word scramble to solve? That would be cool_ That would be amazing_ I love coded messages and scavenger hunts/ hidden passageways and secret things_ Every place is mysterious_ Every place is unknown_ Every place has possibilities_ Even a lonely place_

I/ve spent some time in mental hospitals and I have learned a lot from my experiences there_ I/ll be honest/ they are *so* not glamorous and I hope you never have to see one but every challenging journey holds buried treasure_

In my case I learned a new coping skill_ I was in a group therapy discussion and we were asked to take stock of things that gave us joy/ reasons to go on living_ One woman said/ Geocaching_

Bring the outside in_

I believe in ecotherapy/ that outdoor activities in nature can heal us_ Sometimes our access to beautiful sunny spaces is limited/ however/ so we invite Mother Nature indoors_

Representations of nature can bring comfort and inspiration_ We can still feel the sun and touch the grass of a photograph_ We can take in the beach as we listen to meditative sounds of calm waves_ We can dream on floral sheets_

Here are some other ways to bring the outside in >

Arranging plants and flowers in your home/ even fake ones/ can improve your sense of well–being/ reducing stress and anxiety_ Order beautiful plants online from bloomscape.com_ For fresh flowers/ try a subscription delivery from bouqs.com_ Artificial plants and flowers at aflora.com_

Dogs/ cats/ birds/ fish and other pets ease loneliness/ add purpose/ encourage movement/ lower blood pressure/ reduce stress and anxiety/ help establish new routines and actually increase the production of oxytocin funny foolings_

Bring calm and creativity with fairy garden–ready floral supplies of faux butterflies/ ladybugs/ birds/ bees and more from factorydirect.com_

Listen to the outdoors at home with rich soundscapes on the Calm app featuring everything from crickets to birds to a rainy Paris night_

Tune your computer to full–screen livecams of South African elephants/ Hawaiian beaches/ cat sanctuaries/ aquariums and other nature scenes streaming live at Explore.org_

Add beauty in a bowl and encourage healthier eating with a display of fresh produce_

Mini cacti and hardy succulents from tierrasolstudio.com arrive in handmade ceramic planters and require water only once a month_

Photomurals from wall26.com can transform your bedroom into a lush naturescape from floor to ceiling_

Allposters.com has vintagey travel poster prints for the armchair explorer_ Try the National Parks of the World section_

Bring the outside in_

Try guided meditation and lead your imagination on forest walks or mountain hikes_

Order a collection of floral paintings or prints on Etsy – for less than what you'd spend on a bouquet of real flowers – and add everlasting blooms to any room in your home_

Collage can offer great outside/inside inspiration_ Check bethhoeckel.com for mixed media prints of vintage magazine tears_You'll want to lounge on Lily Pond Lane_

Pitch a pop–up play tent indoors for an instant zen den_ Target/s collab with award–winning illustrator Christian Robinson is a standout_

Consider an indoor water feature_ A tabletop fountain brings beauty and peaceful sound while adding symbolic flow to money/ happiness and love_ Wayfair.com has tons under $100_

A bonsai starter kit comes pre–packaged with all supplies needed to care for a beautiful miniature tree_ Easternleaf.com/s best–seller is a Juniper starter kit_

A waxed Amaryllis bulb requires no care at all yet still delivers incredible blooms_ Tulipworld.com

Healing crystals and stones can be useful to help clear the mind and provide a little guiding light_ Try tinyrituals.co for inspiration_

Try a little patch of fake grass inside and lie on your own personal lawn_

Herbs_

Here/s a little break in programming
to talk about herbs_ Add fresh
herbs to wake up a dish – or even a
simple glass of water – and they/ll
wake you up/ too_ Essential oils can
be especially helpful_

These fragile friends bring small
surprises to the senses_ Take a
moment to breathe them in_

You are cordially invited.

988

Flowers_

Why do I think fresh flowers can help you when you are depressed? It/s probably pretty obvious but/ just in case > they/re beautiful_

They/re fresh they/re green they/re alive_ You care for them_ They care for you_ You replenish water/ trim stems/ shake away faded petals – don/t allow a wilting flower to stay in your arrangements ever cuz it/s a total downer – and each day you observe the wonky architecture of blooms and stems and thorns/ always interesting to look at_ You need nice things to look at_

Are there a lot of nice things to look at/ inspiring things/ in your home and workplace? If so/ good for you_ If not/ consider a simple jar of flowers_ Flowers don/t have to cost much/ don't have to cost anything_ I/ve dumpster–dived for flowers_ I/ve pulled weeds beside the highway_ I/ve chatted up my local florist and asked/ What can I get for ten bucks? Sometimes you can get a lot_ At the very least you/re gonna score a single beautiful flower_One is plenty_ Try it_ Commit to one every week for a month and see_ Who doesn't want to be the kind of person who buys flowers for no reason at all?

Eat your vegs!

Let/s talk about vegetables_ Not here to tell you to eat healthier_ That/s boring_ I/m just encouraging you to spend more time with nature_ Nature is gonna help your mood_ Let/s eat it up_

The CDC reported in 2015 that/ on average/ only 10% of Americans met the official daily serving suggestion of approximately 3 vegetables and 2 fruits_ We are amazing because we are gonna try to grab green at least 3 times a day > something at breakfast/ lunch and dinner_ Easy_ Actually/ if you are like me/ then 3 servings in a day is kinda hard_ Try anyhow_

What is the point of playing this game? The point is just to have a game – a little secret scheme that you play where you have a micro goal and work towards it and then feel a tiny bit good when you achieve it – can be all you need to work your way out of this thing_

The game/ the goal/ is just a distraction_ The fact that it/s good for you is bonus_ Try it_ Have celery with peanut butter_ Grab a wheatgrass shot and drink it down_ Eat fruit_ Try it canned/ dried/ frozen/ chocolate–covered/ though raw is best_ Colorful is best/ also_ Naturally bright colors in food means they are rich in antioxidants/ known to help elevate mood_ Make your plate cheerful to look at and it will be cheerful to eat_

A fun game that I play when at the grocery store is I try to always snag something different from the produce department_ It/s easy to think that this section has the same offerings week after week but this is simply not true_ Look for a variety of tomato that you haven/t yet tried or score some weird fruit_ How often do you purchase kumquats or jicama? What/s there this week that looks strange/ almost inedible? Try it_

Again and again and again I will come back to this suggestion that you try something new_ The experience of taking in a new place/ for example/ feels cognitively different from that of a place you know well/ one you/ll barely examine_ Your eyes move differently/ your mind pursues discovery/ the thoughts you have and the memories you are creating become building blocks/ puzzle pieces/ connected dots_

New experiences/ new tastes/ lead us to questions like/ Where am I? How does this work? but you/re asking it with curiosity/ completely different than when you are sitting at home pondering the sad who/what/when/where/why/s??_ Under the covers on a rainy day such questions feel overwhelming_ Out in the field/ however/ they can be exciting/ like the beginning of a novel_ Ok/ not all surprises are positive – every moment contains risk – but changing it up raises your attention level/ your adrenaline level/ expands your vision of what/s possible_ I want this for you right now_

Try things try things_ Try taking

a big bite out of a serrano pepper and then screaming_ Try unlikely combos of sweet and savory in your salad_ Try roasting vegetables if you never have/ so easy_ Create a self–portrait in mashed potatoes_ Try to perfect an awesome homemade dressing and then salads become sexy_ Spell a help message in carrot sticks and take a picture of it_ One day you might look at it and smile_

Another easy/fun way to score points in the vegetable/fruit game is with smoothies or juices_ I/ve done a few 3/day juice cleanses and they/re pretty interesting/ mostly in the this–is–a–game and trying–something–new kind of way but some people find them very refreshing/ a good reset/ helpful in bringing clarity_ Maybe you will also_

I wouldn/t say that/s been my particular experience/ but I will say I felt a great sense of achievement having lasted 3 days only drinking juice blends of pineapple and kale and beets and ginger_ Good for you and you don/t have to think about food at all for a bit_

Also good because a cleanse gives you some structure/ like you know you gotta have this juice at 5pm/ the next one at 8pm_ Not gonna lie and tell you a juice cleanse is a piece of cake – and it/s definitely not cheap – but I recommend trying sometime/ just for the experience_

So we/ve talked about eating and drinking produce but let/s not forget there are all sorts of enriching ways to experience it as well_ Put the farmers market schedule into your calendar_ You need to go there_ Make a friend arrange an apple or berry picking adventure_ Fill that fruit bowl_ Make jam_ Forage_

Depressed? Try >

bananas

The most popular fruit in the United States/ bananas contain 20% of the recommended daily allowance of vitamin B6_ Vitamin B6 helps your body create serotonin = hello good mood! and melatonin = great sleep! Bananas are also high in potassium_ Science asserts that people who eat a diet rich in potassium have less depressive symptoms_

broccoli

The high amounts of chromium found in broccoli actually increase brain chemicals related to positive feelings/ energy and memory_ Researchers have also found that broccoli helps fight depression_

oranges

The mere act of smelling an orange can energize your mood while eating oranges < also lemons/ limes and grapefruit > can have cognitive benefits_ A study in the UK found that drinking orange juice over an eight–week period brought measurable mood–boosting benefits_

greens

Leafy greens like lettuce/ spinach/ swiss chard and arugula contain folate/ another serotonin boosting B vitamin_ Low folate levels can lead to depressive symptoms and poor response to antidepressants_ Also/ leafy greens are an important part of the Mediterranean diet_ Research shows that people following this diet enjoy happier and healthier lives_

apples

Apples are a terrific source of pectin/ an essential fiber found in fruit and vegetables_ Studies have determined that high amounts of fiber means a lower risk of depression_ Pectin has additional benefits when it comes to gut bacteria_ Recent research asserts a connection between the gut microbiome and depression_

mushrooms

A serving of mushrooms can equal a D vitamin supplement_ Vitamin D lowers blood pressure/ improves bone health/ even reduces the risk of heart disease/ but is perhaps best known for its role in producing serotonin_

carrots

The orange pigment in carrots, squash, and sweet potatoes comes from carotenoids/ a type of antioxidant that can help fight depression_ One study revealed a connection between greater blood levels of carotenoids and optimism_

blueberries

Blueberries are good for the brain_ According to Psychiatric Times/ blueberries are the number one superfood that can ease symptoms of depression_ Thanks to antioxidants known as flavonoids/ berries help activate neural pathways associated with cognition and mood_ Same goes for strawberries/ raspberries/ and blackberries/ all packed with vitamin C_

avocados

Did you know that technically an avocado is a fruit? Avocados are rich in stress–relieving B vitamins and omega–3 which is good for mood and brain health_

I asked friends to share the best advice they ever received about weathering hard times_

→

You are right where you are supposed to be_

Someone sent this to me once when I was in a very difficult time in my life/ and it made me stop and think that there was a reason_

Don/t try to fix a temporary problem with a permanent solution_

Sometimes I put a reminder on my calendar to check in in a week to see if I feel differently_ I always feel differently_ Not always better_ But usually not worse_

Remember that feelings are only temporary_ They will pass_

My therapist says/

^Everything you need is already inside you_^

I always feel better when she tells me that_

No rain/ no flowers_

I asked friends to share the best advice they ever received about weathering hard times_

→

Take it one day at a time_

I use a reframing process a lot_ What is the story I/m telling myself? How does it feel? What is it surfacing in me that needs attention? How would I reframe this if I were speaking to a friend?

A friend bluntly said/^ No one knows what the fuck they/re doing/ so don/t get hung up thinking you/re doing it wrong_^ A good reminder that we/re all stumbling through this world trying to make sense of it.

The only way out is through_
My dad would say that to me_

Sometimes things are just going to suck/ but then eventually/ hopefully/ they won/t_

Best advice? Take a nap_
Get some rest_
Go to bed_ Figure it out tomorrow_
Sometimes you want to fix it or
figure it out or overthink it_

Weather_ You even used
the word ^weathering^_ The
advice was to imagine weather –
storms come and pass through/
overcast months give way to
clearer skies/ sunny days can
shift to the weight of thick humid
air but cool breezes will come
again and lift the weight_ As a
farmer who watches the weather
frequently/ this analogy really
resonates_ We can't control
the weather/ it influences us/
including our emotional states/
but it always changes_

It/s ok
to cry_

When you're
going through
hell, keep going.
This really helped because it
kept me in motion emotionally
and physically/ never staying
in the depths of the despair
for too long, always letting it
pass me by as I continued on
my journey_

I think a lot about
the wisdom
of taking a
counteraction_
For instance/ if I feel afraid/,
I behave as if I/m brave_ If I am
angry at someone/ I try to do
something loving for them_
And so on_ _ _

Don/t be a
douchebag_
Solid advice LOL

Luck_

Let/s consider the four–leaf clover_ A friend of mine gave me one when I was terribly depressed_ It was laminated on a card/ a five–leaf clover in fact/ one she had found in 1987_ And she gave it to *me*_ Did I believe then that four–leaf clovers were lucky? Not especially/ until that moment_ Suddenly I possessed a rare and magic gift_

Yet with it came important consequences > ^Keep this safe^/ she wrote/ ^cuz I/ll need you to return it if I ever fall on hard times_^ I know maybe this wasn/t the intended message but what I heard in it was my friend saying/ You can/t kill yourself cuz I/m gonna need this back_ I now had important responsibilities/ stewardship__

I want to talk about luck because/

my friend/ you deserve it_ Of course you can/t wish depression away – small/ positive actions will have the greatest impact – but I don/t think it hurts to invite a rainbow here and there to help out_

What/s something you imagine might have magical properties? Ladybugs or maneki-neko or white peacocks? Doesn/t have to be a classic good luck symbol many agree upon_ Horseshoes and shooting stars might not connect for you_ Merely consider something you love/ something you think has mystery/

has It_ And then what could be wrong with surrounding yourself with more of It?

We can make our own luck_ Just invite it in_ Eat Lucky Charms for breakfast_ Place a photo of a beautiful fountain near where you toss your change and make a wish each time_ Wear a vintage charm bracelet_ Set your alarm for 11:11_ Having a small ritual or lucky item invites hope/ affirms that we all deserve – and get – lucky breaks in life. We never know when they will come but/ trust me/ they will_

Playlist +

Artist Kate Bingaman–Burt illustrated the work you see here – part of her Other People/s Plants series – and also made a mixtape for us! Check out our latest Spotify playlist for her fresh soundtrack to this chapter > spoti.fi/3s4fZno_ For more KBB visit @katebingburt

Tell us about the playlist!
I curated songs with titles incorporating weather/ growing/ vegetables/ fruit/ and seasons from a bunch of my already created playlists_ Plus/ a song that is titled ^Buddy^ because of you! LOL :)

What is Other People/s Plants?
Other People/s Plants is an ongoing drawing series where I draw other people's plants! I started this series years ago with my plants and then moved on to drawing submissions of other people/s plants_ I made a few prints as well as a currently out–of–print zine_ Sadly/ all of the plants from this series have died/ but I still have the drawings!

What did you learn from drawing Other People's Plants?
Honestly/ this was the beginning of me exploring pattern and linework in my drawing practice_ Plants were the perfect subject to focus on pattern and line in nature as well as an excellent subject to inject imaginary pattern and line_ I also really enjoyed hearing stories from folks about their beloved plant friends_

Can you tell us about a difficult time and how you got through it?
Drawing/ baby! Drawing always makes me feel better_ It/s equal to meditation_ I slow down/ am by myself/ focus on the subject and my breathing/ and make something all at the same time_ Drawing is my meditation/ and it helps me through big stresses and the little ones_

A'S

XEL'S

ANNA'S

JUDITH'S

ZACH'S

NN'S

CHAR

Here are two trees with mad branches: one with the branches pointing downwards, one with them going up.

Drawing
a tree_

In 1978 the Italian designer and
artist Bruno Munari published a slim
volume titled simply *Drawing a Tree_*
Bruno Munari proposes > ^When
drawing a tree/ always remember
that every branch is more slender
than the one that came before_ Also
note that the trunk splits into two
branches/ then those branches split in
two/ then those in two/ and so on/ and
so on/ until you have a full tree/ be it
straight/ squiggly/ curved up/ curved
down/ or bent sideways by the wind_^
I think drawing could help your
mood. Try it_

Spring cleaning_

Spring cleaning doesn/t only happen in the spring/ of course you know this_ Spring cleaning can happen anytime you want_ Just adding the word ^spring^ before ^cleaning^ rebrands it instantly more fresh_ Spring cleaning is getting ready for a new season/ a new you_

So I/m thinking you need a *small* cleaning or organizing project_ Try reviewing your shoes/ eliminating ones you won/t likely wear and then setting them in a nice/ neat row_ Over the next couple days you/ll spy that row and notice how nice/ neat

it is_ You did that_ You can bring order to anything you want_ You can make anything better_ When you are depressed everything feels wrong/ out of place/ overwhelming_ Just take a half hour and prove this isn't so.

When I was in an outpatient program/ which is like a part–time mental health day camp that you typically land in after a full–time stay in the hospital/ lots of people talked about this_ People would come in on a Monday and share their weekend challenges and minor joys of reassembling their lives – unopened piles of mail full of past–due bills/ tax documents/ legal papers/ unread magazines – and always it seemed tackling the worst/ most boring-est/ dreaded chores/ even for five minutes/ brought a bit of hope/ of putting it back together_

I took on my closet_ I would spend an early morning hour a day on it/ though if you saw how tiny my closet was and how minimal its contents were you would think I could have organized it in under an hour_ You would have been right/ on

Spring cleaning_

a good day_ But/ at that particular place in my life/ it took me five_ I/m not embarrassed about it_ I took the time that I needed/ a little bit each day/ and it helped me feel good_

Some ideas of things you could try for 20 minutes that might help you feel good/ too > Clean out your refrigerator_ Just go in there and remove anything past the expiration date_ Get rid of old jars of pickles_ Reorganize a little/ spritz some cleaner in there/ zoom across it with a paper towel and suddenly you might find yourself just a little more inspired to grocery shop_

Or > find one shelf in a bookshelf and reorder the books by size/ smallest on left and moving up towards the largest on the right/ always going up/ up/ never down/ because it/s more optimistic that way_ Grab one drawer in a dresser/ just one/ and take everything out of it/ write a tiny note to Future You in the botton of the drawer – one time I wrote simply/ ^It/s ok^ – then neatly return only the contents you love_ Donate the rest_

Omg/ the medicine cabinet_ When/s the last time you looked at it and placed something special inside/ next to the deo? Set a crystal in there or a pair of Barbie shoes_ Simple upgrade > Wash out some of those jars you emptied from the fridge and use /em to hold toothbrushes/ cotton balls/ Q-tips_

Alert! Though I/m talking up small yet bold edits to your living space/ please do not begin in a spot full of sentimental things/ like if you keep old journals under your bed/ don/t go near that crap > too emotional_ Stick to the facts/ Jack/ and start simple_ It/s gonna make you feel great_

Sometimes I find organizing can get agonizing when I begin to worry about how to donate stuff_ A great solution to this is the ever–awesome Free Box/ so fun_ Set a cardboard box on the street labeled F/RE/E with your junk inside/ walk down to the local park for a cleaning break and then come back and laugh to yourself at all that/s already taken_ Helping others is fun_

Of course here I/m going to recommend Marie Kondo/s *The Life–Changing Magic of Tidying Up_* This is a great book! What you are doing right now *is* magic. So recycle those old newspapers/ get rid of gifts you don/t like_ What else are you holding onto that you can now let go of?

Shopping

Annie Poon

I like spending money_ I think it/s fun and I/m going to suggest it here as an antidepressant_ Doesn/t have to be a lot/ just buy yourself a little something to make your life better/ more enjoyable > a meaningful book/ a new coffee mug/ a candle/ a sketchbook/ a trophy from the junk shop_ Retail therapy is good_

An investigative pick–me–up stroll through the drugstore could have you trying cute travel–size brands of toiletries you/d normally never consider_ If health food stores are more your scene/ let's chat up Dr. Bronner soaps_ I doubt you have tried every variety and you can purchase an 8oz of liquid soap for a mere $6_ This classic product offers bold/invigorating scent therapy plus weird fine print everywhere celebrating the late Dr. Bronner/s inspired ALL–ONE! philosophy which is pretty awesome_

Hold it_ Stop_ Do *not* do this shopping on the internet_ I say this – and I used to own an online store/ people – because shopping in person enhances the potential benefits of this mood–turnaround experiment_ You have to walk/ drive/ take public trans to your retail establishment of choice so that gets you out a tiny bit/ inspires some movement/ kinda like exercise_ And then/ even if you are merely buying a new Chapstick/ you have to interact with people along the way/ also a good thing_

This is the yellow chapter of Rainbows. It's the funnest, coolest book about depression.

te it
f   u.

Buddy

Rainbows. The funnest, coolest book about beating depression.

So far we have four chapters in the *Rainbows* series besides this one_ I/m gonna attempt to tell you a little about each so maybe you/ll check /em out >> The black chapter was the first one/ felt right to start in the dark_ It also borrows the black of a pen or pencil and talks about writing and drawing as mood turnaround skills_ Everything from gratitude journaling to making lists/ writing can be super helpful_ Don/t think you/re a writer? Neither do I but I keep trying_ You can/ too_ Same with drawing_ I can/t draw but sometimes I try with a friend and it/s really fun_ The chapter has tons of cool downloads and also talks about time travel/ using a timer to push yourself further/ setting a mere 5–minute intention to do something you don/t want to_ Blue came next and that chapter is especially focused on getting help/ with a bunch of therapies to try and also explores the healing power of swimming and skydiving_ Pink talks tons about exercise_ On the opposite side of the spectrum is baking_ Some find great comfort in baking and cooking so that/s a mindfulness exercise that/s worth a try/ _ Plus a 30sec trick to fight obsessive thoughts_ And then yellow is a sunny chapter/ talking about the importance of sunlight/ yellow flowers/ lemons/ Nancy Drew_ Just want you to be open to possibilities of mystery/ of not knowing but hoping_ Not knowing but having faith that things can turn around_ They can and they will_ All four books are available on Amazon_

I'm so glad
you're
alive.

Annie Poon

Emergency Resources >

call/text 988

Suicide and Crisis Lifeline

Up
next>
purple